THREE SIDES
and the
ROUND ONE

By Margaret Friskey

Illustrated by Mary Gehr

 CHILDRENS PRESS, CHICAGO

Library of Congress Cataloging in Publication Data

Friskey, Margaret, 1901-
  Three sides and the round one.

  SUMMARY: A discussion between a circle and a triangle
introduces basic geometric shapes and suggests where they
can be found in common objects.
  [1. Geometry. 2. Size and shape] I. Gehr, Mary,
illus. II. Title.
PZ8.3.F9179Th   [E]   72-8347
ISBN 0-516-03627-0

1 2 3 4 5 6 7 8 9 10 11 12 13 14 15 16 17 18 19 20 21 22 23 24 25 R 75 74 73

"You good-for-nothing Three-sides!" said the Round One.

Look at me!

I am the eyes
of an owl,

the yellow moon,

4

a rubber ball,

a big balloon.

Round, all around,
all around!

5

Round as a cookie.

Round as a wheel.

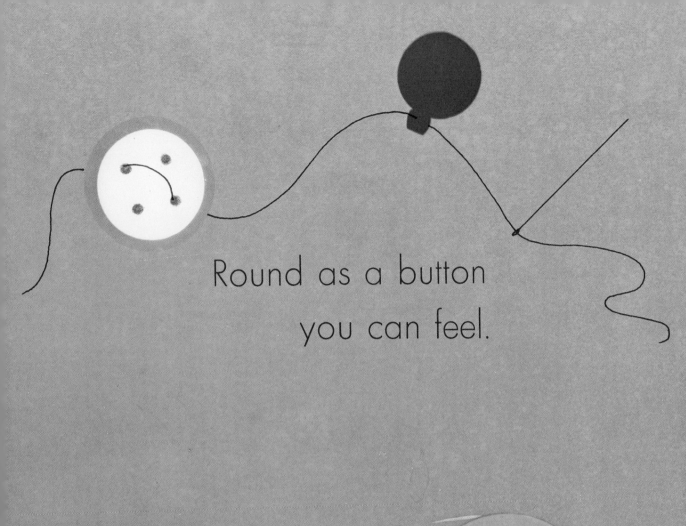

Round as a button
you can feel.

Call me CIRCLE.

Call me SPHERE.
Round, all around,
all around!

I have friends
with rounded ends.

Call them OVAL.

See them in mittens
and kittens,

and cat eyes as well.

See them
in fishes

and dishes

and eggs in the shell.

"You good-for-nothing Three-sides,"

said the Round One.

Four-sides has more sides.

There!
Call him SQUARE.

See him
in tables,

and labels,

16

or the back
of a chair.

GRAPE
JELLY

pop
corn

He's ever
so clever.
He's the side
of a CUBE.

This puts him
on blocks,

and on sides of
a box.

Four-sides has a brother,
Long-sides.

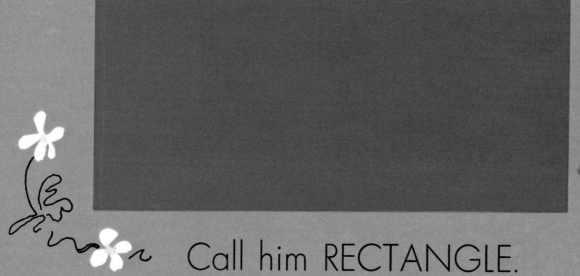

Call him RECTANGLE.

See him
 in windows,

and doorways,

and even
in more ways.

Thick as a brick,
he is still
RECTANGULAR.

"I go places
with Long-sides,"
said the Round One,

"as a wagon,

a scooter,

a car
on a train.''

"Just a minute,
you wise eyes
of an owl,"
said Three-sides.
"I am his beak.
Look at me!
Look at me!

I am a sail,

a kite,

the peak of a roof.

That is proof
of my importance.

Call me TRIANGLE."

"Very well," said
the Round One.

"It takes all shapes
to make a world."

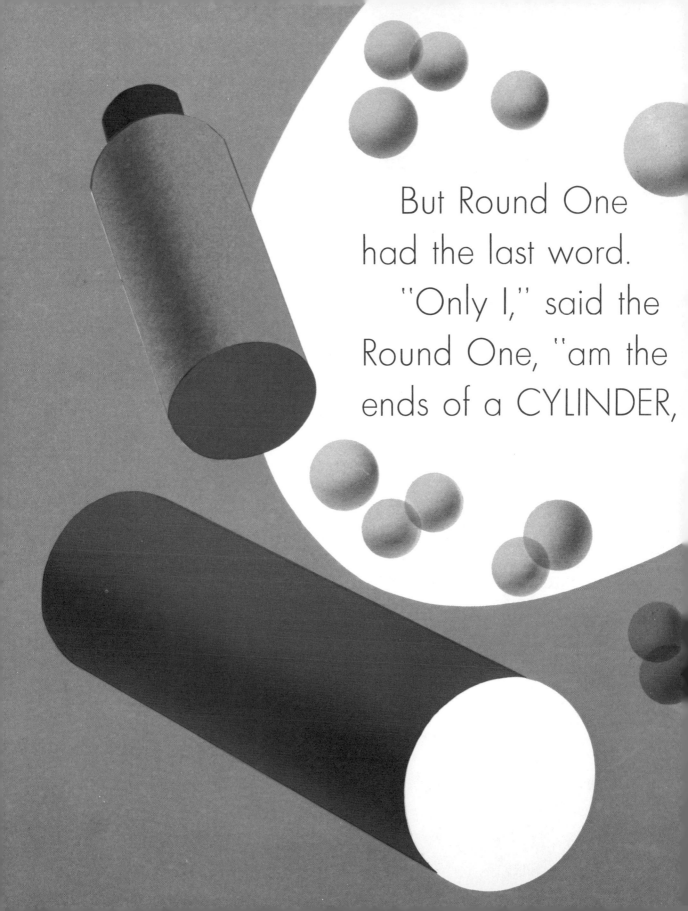

But Round One
had the last word.
"Only I," said the
Round One, "am the
ends of a CYLINDER,

and the base of a CONE.

I alone
am round, all around,
all around!"

SHAPES TO SEE EVERY DAY

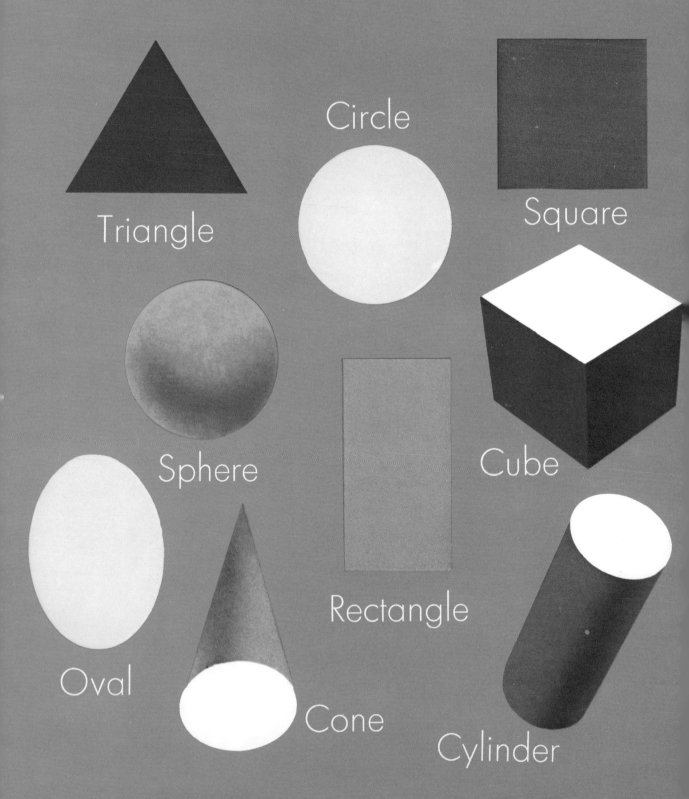

Triangle

Circle

Square

Sphere

Rectangle

Cube

Oval

Cone

Cylinder